MICHEL ROUX

sauces for savory dishes

Dedication

To my son Alain, who cooks side-by-side with me at The Waterside Inn.

Contents

Foreword

This special category of sauces covers a wide spectrum of ingredients and comes in a vast palette of colors, from yellow ocher to dark mahogany. All are iridescent and lustrous, with the limpidity of water from a mountain spring. Their subtle aromas vary according to their composition and the desired effect. They are all sublime: some, like game sauces, are potent, and all are conducive to conviviality. These sauces are more structured, aromatic, and muscular, and have a far longer finish in the mouth than those for fish and shellfish, since they are designed to accompany meat.

The great classic sauces, like Périgueux and Bordelaise Sauce, are based on veal stock. They need longer, more complicated preparation, but the effort involved is amply repaid by the enormous pleasure they give your guests, who will appreciate your mastery of the art of sauce-making.

You will be amazed when you discover the sweet, astringent sauces which are my particular favorites. Bigarade Sauce, for example, strikes your tongue like a gentle whiplash. This sauce is perfect served with calves' liver, or duck *magrets*, or braised veal tongue.

I have a childhood memory of Maman's ritual Wednesday simmering of a Charcutière Sauce for our lunch. While the sauce was cooking, she would brown some middle-neck pork chops (one of the cheapest cuts you can buy, but also one of the most tender and tasty) in the frying pan. When the chops were cooked to perfection, they exuded a few droplets of juice and were then ready to be coated in the sauce. Perched on a stool, clutching a small knife, I would cut the cornichons into long strips under the watchful and loving eye of my mother. I was so proud when my cornichons were mixed into Maman's sauce! I would rush to be at the table before anyone else, insisting that I had the first serving of the potato purée which she always made with this dish. Quickly, I made a well in the middle and eagerly held out my plate for her to pour in the sauce. The *mélange* of purée and sauce sent me into a transport of delight and I could not eat my pork chop until I had been completely engulfed by it (and, of course, begged for a touch more sauce).

Things have changed, however. Nowadays at The Waterside Inn, sauce-making is like a ballet—one dance for my delicate pan-fried poultry, another for my roast Scotch beef, and yet another for my Welsh baby lamb *en croûte*, not forgetting the excellent and abundant game we get from numerous English shoots. Under my conductor's baton, the orchestra of sauce chefs devote their attention to preparing the sauces: purifying, skimming, slowing down, or accelerating the cooking, inhaling the aroma and admiring their own reflections in the stockpot before straining the finished product through a cheesecloth or a fine conical sieve. At the climax, they season the sauces to perfection and present each one to me in a tiny pan for my approval. They have danced to my tune and I, the maestro, add the final flourish by carefully pouring the sauce in a ribbon around the meat on the plate just before it leaves the kitchen. And in the dining room the sound of applause is heard as the ballet of sauces comes to its conclusion. What a marvellous aroma, and what a feast for the eyes!

About Stocks

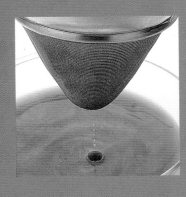

Stocks are the very foundation of sauces; on their quality depends the sucess of your sauces and your mastery of sauce-making.

• All the ingredients must be extremely fresh and of the highest quality.

• Equally important: do not drown the stock at the outset by adding too much water to the ingredients; it will make it tasteless and watery. If necessary you can always add more cold water later.

• Always add cold water to a stock. Hot water will make it cloudy and you will lose the desired crystal clarity.

• Cooking a stock for longer does not make it better—quite the reverse. Long cooking can actually be detrimental, since the stock becomes heavy and loses its flavor. Follow the cooking times in the recipes precisely.

• For a double depth of flavor, cook the stock twice, using cold water the first time, and the cooled batch of stock the second time.

• In essence, stocks are embryonic sauces, which must be carefully nurtured and titivated. They should be cooked at a simmer and never allowed to boil, and must be skimmed and degreased regularly to remove all impurities. Finally,.they must be strained gently and delicately through a wire-mesh conical sieve, taking care not to cloud their clarity.

About Sauces

The great sauces

The great classics have been around for centuries. Noble, powerful, aristocratic, and elegant, they form part of our heritage. These are sauces fit for feast days and special occasions.

The lesser sauces

There are multitudes of these, suitable for any occasion and every day. They can be prepared in a matter of moments, with very little effort, to complement a piece of meat, poultry, or game.

The basic elements

All sauces, however simple or complex, should be based on good-quality ingredients. Aromatics, fresh herbs, spices, wines, alcohol, stocks—all must be chosen with the utmost care.

The bartender

A sauce-maker is like a bartender mixing cocktails. It is vital to get the proportions right. Ingredients with a very strong flavor, like certain pungent spices, herbs, and alcohol, should be used in moderation.

The cook as alchemist

A pinch of this, a pinch of that—the creative process is bewitching. A flame licks up from the pan containing the bubbling, steaming potion, illuminating the sagacious face of the "saucerer." He inhales the fumes laden with the first aromas. His imagination is fired as he conjures up the magic of his sauce.

My sauces

From the age of fourteen, during my apprenticeship to a *pâtissier*, followed by many years in professional kitchens, I learned the secret of sauces, from the chefs with whom I worked. Later, I developed them to suit my own palate and created original new sauces to complement my dishes.

There are sauces to suit every season, every taste, every occasion, and the time available for their preparation. My objective when making a sauce, be it savory or sweet, is to provide the perfect accompaniment to a dish and to elevate it to gastronomic perfection—but never to dominate it.

In the course of a year at The Waterside Inn, I prepare hundreds of different sauces—modern, classic, light, or unctuous, depending on the dish they are to accompany. Those in this book are among my favorites. They are creative and diverse, enormously enjoyable, and perfectly accessible to the home cook.

Cooking a sauce intoxicates the senses of smell, taste, and sight. The visual and odiferous pleasures it offers in its final cooking stages will tempt you to dream and discover the wonderful world of sauces.

Practical Advice

Choosing & flavoring sauces

Menu planning: Serve only one "grand" sauce at a meal and keep the others light and simple.

Do not serve a powerful, full-bodied sauce at the beginning of a meal.

Try to avoid serving sauces of the same color and texture, or with a similar base, such as wine or liqueurs.

Do not make all the sauces at the same meal too classic or too modern. Your guests will appreciate a judicious balance.

Seasonal produce: In the same way that you would choose the finest seasonal ingredients for a finished dish, make your sauces with the best seasonal produce. The end result will be full of flavor and all the more delicious.

Seasoning: Never add too much salt to a sauce before it has reached the desired consistency and taste. Add pepper only just before serving to retain its flavor and zip.

Garlic: Always halve garlic cloves lengthwise and remove the green shoot, which can be indigestible.

Mushrooms: Their wild, musky aroma of forest bark and damp earth adds a special something to many sauces. It is better to wipe fresh mushrooms clean than to wash them, as they absorb water and lose their flavor. Chop or finely slice them and add to the sauce during cooking. Some varieties, such as common mushrooms, tend to lack flavor, so be generous with these. Others, such as shiitake, have quite an aggressive flavor and should be used sparingly. Dried mushrooms are a good

To crush garlic, put the peeled cloves in a mortar with a large pinch of coarse salt

Crush the garlic to a paste with a pestle

substitute for fresh (soak them first). For the ultimate pleasure, black or white truffles can be added to numerous sauces a few minutes before serving.

Shallots: Shallots become bitter after chopping, so rinse them under cold water before using in a sauce.

Vinegar and lemon: A few drops of vinegar or lemon juice added to a characterless sauce just before serving will pep up the taste.

Preparing, keeping, and freezing sauces

Preparation time: The preparation times given in this book are based on ingredients that have already been measured and prepared as indicated in the ingredients list. They do not include the time taken to peel, chop, slice, or blanch vegetables or bones, soften butter, etc, or any necessary cooling time.

Cooking time: The timings given for cooking and reducing sauces are intended only as guidelines, since the degree of heat will vary depending on your stove and the type of saucepan used. The only infallible way to ensure that a sauce has reached the desired consistency is to check it on the back of a spoon.

Degreasing: The easiest way to degrease a stock is to let it cool completely at room temperature, then refrigerate it. The fat will solidify on the surface and can be carefully lifted off with a large spoon.

Deglazing: Liquid such as wine or stock is heated with the cooking juices and sediment left in the pan after roasting or pan-frying to make a sauce or gravy. Remove most of the fat and grease from the pan before adding the liquid.

Straining: Thin sauces can be passed straight through a conical sieve. Thicker sauces should be pushed through the sieve by pressing with the back of a ladle or twisting a small whisk.

Keeping sauces warm: A *bain-marie* is best for this. Use a saucepan large enough to hold the pan or bowl containing the sauce, and fill the pan with hot water.

Dot flakes of butter over the surface of white sauces to prevent a skin from forming. Sauces that need a liaison or "smoothing" with butter should be kept in the *bain-marie*, and the liaison or butter added at the moment of serving.

Hot emulsion sauces: These sauces do not like to be kept waiting. To enjoy them at their delicate best, make them at the last possible moment and serve immediately.

Herbs and spices

In Bray, I have created an herb garden on the banks of the Thames. Every day in the summer months, I painstakingly and parsimoniously pick the numerous different herbs I need for my sauces and salads. Freshness is a vital factor in the success of a sauce, and my herb garden is my trump card.

If you use dried herbs, keep them in airtight jars in a cool, dark place. Spices lose their color and flavor if they are kept too long; you should throw away any open jars after 3–6 months because the spice will add nothing to your sauces, and may even spoil them.

To flavor a sauce with peppercorns, crush them and place on a piece of cheesecloth

Fold up the edges to make a purse and tie with string

The golden rules for using herbs and spices

- Small quantities but good quality.
- Do not mix contradictory and powerful flavors.

If you obey these rules, you will discover a wonderful world of flavors—subtle, complex, musky, fresh, spicy, and delectable.

Bouquet garni: A classic bouquet garni consists of a sprig of thyme, a bay leaf, and parsley stems wrapped and tied in a leek leaf.

Fines herbes: A mixture of fresh herbs in equal quantities: chervil, chives, parsley, and tarragon. They should be snipped, not chopped, preferably only a short time before using so that they retain the maximum flavor and do not become bitter.

The most popular culinary herbs are: basil, bay leaf, chervil, chives, cilantro, dill, fennel, garlic, horseradish, lavender, lemon grass, lemon verbena, lovage, marjoram, mint, oregano, flat or curly parsley, rosemary, sage, savory, sorrel, tarragon, and thyme.

The most popular spices are: caraway, cardamom, cayenne, cinnamon, cloves, coriander seeds, cumin, curry, five-spice, ginger, juniper, mace, nutmeg, peppercorns (black, green, white, and pink), paprika, pimento, poppy seeds, saffron, and star anise.

Dairy products

These play an extremely important part in sauce-making.

Crème fraîche: This can be heated to not more than 175°F, after which it will separate. To use it in a hot sauce, whisk it into the sauce off the heat, without further cooking. This slightly acidulated cream is light and refreshing and is delicious added to most cold sauces.

Heavy cream: This tolerates heat extremely well during cooking and can even be reduced by boiling. It is often used as a liaison, but above all it makes sauces creamy and velvety.

Hard cheeses: The most important and best are Parmesan, Gruyère, Emmenthal, and Cheddar. I always buy medium-aged farmhouse cheeses, which have a full, sublime flavor. These cheeses are usually used freshly grated to finish a sauce. It takes a few minutes after they have been added for their savor to develop, so you should use them judiciously and parsimoniously at first, checking their development before adding more to the sauce.

Do not use cheap, poor-quality cheese, which can ruin a sauce by tasting rancid, soapy, or too salty.

Roquefort: My noble Lord Roquefort will acquire star status in a salad dressing, a cold sauce for *crudités,* and certain hot sauces. I adore Roquefort. Used in moderation, it creates an explosion of different savors in a sauce. Bleu d'Auvergne and Fourme d'Ambert make adequate substitutes, but cannot equal the real thing.

Unsalted butter: The finest of all dairy products. It is natural and healthy and practically indispensable in the kitchen. Its delicate taste and different complexities vary according to its provenance and origins. It adds the finishing touch to many of my sauces, but I always use it in moderation. I use only unsalted butter in my cooking. This is essential for making clarified butter and desirable for all sauces.

At The Waterside Inn, after many blind tastings, the butter I have chosen for the table and for my *beurres blancs* and sauces is the *appellation contrôlée* Echiré from the Deux-Sèvres. Its quality and value place it among the very best French butters.

When either unsalted and salted butter is melted, its components separate into 15—20% water, 4% protein, and the balance butterfat.

Veal Stock

Veal stock makes brown sauces delicate and well-balanced, without masking their individuality.

Makes 1 quart
Preparation time: *30 minutes*
Cooking time: *about 3 hours*

Ingredients:

3¼ pounds veal bones, chopped
½ calf's foot, split lengthwise,
chopped, and blanched
2 carrots, cut in rounds
⅔ cup coarsely chopped onion
1 cup dry white wine
1 celery stalk, thinly sliced
6 tomatoes, peeled, seeded,
and chopped
2 cups thinly sliced button
mushrooms
2 garlic cloves
1 bouquet garni (page 11),
including a sprig of tarragon

Preheat the oven to 425°F. Put the veal bones and calf's foot in a roasting pan and brown in the oven, turning them from time to time with a slotted spoon. When they have browned, add the carrots and onion, mix together, and cook for 5 minutes longer. Using the slotted spoon, transfer all the contents of the roasting pan to a large saucepan or casserole. Pour off the fat from the roasting pan and deglaze with the white wine, scraping up all the sediment. Set over high heat and reduce by half, then pour the wine into the saucepan. Add 3 quarts cold water and bring to a boil over high heat. As soon as the liquid boils, reduce the heat so that the surface is barely trembling. Simmer for 10 minutes, then skim well and add all the other ingredients.

Simmer the stock, uncovered, for 2½ hours, skimming as necessary. Strain through a fine-mesh conical sieve into a bowl and cool over ice (see page 14).

Demi-glace or glace: Reduce the strained stock by one-third to make a *demi-glace*; reduce by half for a *glace*. These *glaces* enhance sauces, adding moistness and a fuller flavor. But they cannot add finesse and subtlety, since the lengthy cooking time involved destroys some of their delicate flavor and aroma.

Chicken Stock

I sometimes add half a veal shank, when preparing this stock, which makes it extra rich and unctuous. Like all stocks, it should be cooled as quickly as possible. The best way to do this is to plunge the saucepan into a bowl of ice cubes until the stock is completely cold.

Ingredients:

1 stewing chicken, weighing 3¼ pounds,
or an equal weight of chicken carcasses
or wings, blanched and refreshed

2 carrots, cut in chunks

White part of 2 leeks, cut in chunks

1 celery stalk, coarsely chopped

1 onion, studded with 2 cloves

2 cups thinly sliced button mushrooms

1 bouquet garni (page 11

Makes about 1½ quarts

Preparation time: **15 minutes**

Cooking time: **about 1 hour 45 minutes**

Put the chicken or carcasses in a saucepan and cover with 2½ quarts cold water. Bring to a boil over high heat, then immediately lower the heat and keep at a simmer. After 5 minutes, skim the surface and add all the other ingredients. Cook gently for 1½ hours, without boiling, skimming whenever necessary.

Strain the stock through a wire-mesh conical sieve and cool it as quickly as possible over a bowl of ice.

Chicken Velouté

This velouté *can be used as a base for other sauces; just omit the sherry. Personally, I find it excellent just as it is. I serve it with poached poultry and rice or with a whole pan-fried veal sweetbread garnished with leaf spinach.*

Ingredients:

¼ cup white roux, hot (page 22)

3 cups chicken stock, cooled (above)

¼ cup dry sherry (optional)

Salt and freshly ground white pepper

Serves 6 (makes about 3½ cups)

Preparation time: **5 minutes**

Cooking time: **about 30 minutes**

Put the hot white roux into a saucepan and add the cold chicken stock. Set over medium heat and bring to a boil, whisking continuously. Reduce the heat and gently simmer the *velouté* for 30 minutes, stirring the sauce and skimming the surface every 10 minutes. Add the sherry if you are using it, and cook for 1 more minute. Season the sauce with salt and white pepper, and pass it through a wire-mesh conical sieve.

Game Stock

This stock makes the perfect sauce for pan-fried noisettes of venison. Deglaze the pan with port wine, add a teaspoon of red-currant jelly, then add the game stock. Whisk in a small piece of butter and season to taste. Delicious!

Ingredients:

3 tablespoons peanut oil

4 pounds game trimmings, carcasses, necks, wings, etc, cut in pieces

2 small carrots, cut in rounds

1 cup coarsely chopped onions

½ head of garlic, halved widthwise

2 cups red wine (preferably Côtes du Rhône)

2 cups veal stock (page 12)

8 juniper berries, crushed

8 coriander seeds, crushed

1 bouquet garni (page 11), including 2 sage leaves and a celery stalk

Makes 1½ quarts

Preparation time: 30 minutes

Cooking time: 2 hours 15 minutes

Preheat the oven to 425°F. Heat the oil in a roasting pan, then put in the game carcasses or trimmings and brown in the hot oven, turning them from time to time with a slotted spoon. When the meat has browned, add the carrots, onions, and garlic, mix together, and cook for 5 minutes longer. With the slotted spoon, transfer all the contents of the roasting pan to a large saucepan or casserole. Pour off the fat from the roasting pan and deglaze with the red wine. Set over high heat and reduce the wine by half, then pour it into the saucepan. Add 2 quarts cold water and bring to a boil over high heat. As soon as the liquid boils, reduce the heat so that the surface barely trembles. Simmer for 10 minutes, then skim well and add all the other ingredients.

Simmer the stock, uncovered, for 2 hours, skimming the surface as necessary. Strain it through a fine-mesh conical sieve into a bowl and cool as quickly as possible over a bowl of ice.

Once the stock has been strained, you can reduce it by one-third to give it more body. Like all stocks, it will keep well for several days in the refrigerator, or for three or four months in the freezer.

Lamb Stock

This lamb stock is light in both flavor and appearance. I use it for deglazing in many roasted or pan-fried lamb recipes, such as a navarin. It can form the basis for a sauce, in which case I would flavor it with curry, star anise, mint, or saffron, etc to complement the dish. For a wonderful taste of spring, I sometimes use the stock to moisten a couscous garnished with tender young vegetables.

Ingredients:

3¼ pounds neck or shoulder of lamb, skin and fat removed cut in pieces

2 small carrots, cut in rounds

⅔ cup coarsely chopped onion

1 cup dry white wine

4 tomatoes, peeled, seeded, and chopped

2 garlic cloves

1 bouquet garni (page 11), including 2 sprigs of tarragon and a celery stalk

6 white peppercorns, crushed

Makes 1 quart

*Preparation time: **30 minutes***

*Cooking time: **about 2 hours***

Preheat the oven to 425°F. Put the pieces of lamb in a roasting pan and brown in the hot oven, turning them over from time to time with a slotted spoon. When the lamb has colored, add the carrots and onions, mix together, and cook for 5 minutes longer. Still using the slotted spoon, transfer all the contents of the roasting pan to a large saucepan or casserole. Pour off the fat from the roasting pan, deglaze with the white wine, and reduce by half. Pour the reduced wine into the saucepan, add 2½ quarts cold water, and bring to a boil over high heat. As soon as the liquid boils, reduce the heat so that the surface is barely trembling. Simmer for 10 minutes, then skim the surface and add all the other ingredients.

Simmer, uncovered, for 1½ hours, skimming the surface as necessary. Strain the stock through a fine-mesh conical sieve into a bowl and cool it as quickly as possible over a bowl of ice.

Cooked Marinade

Large pieces of meat or game can be left in the cold marinade for one to three days; smaller pieces should be marinated for one or two hours. If you plan to serve the meat the same day, it can be placed in the marinade while this is still warm. Always use tongs or a fork to turn the meat in the marinade, never your fingers, which will spoil it.

The addition of a small amount of marinade to a game sauce will reinforce its structure and flavor.

Ingredients:

1½ tablespoons butter

2 carrots, cut in rounds

2 onions, roughly chopped

1 celery stalk, thinly sliced

1 quart red wine (preferably Côtes du Rhône)

7 tablespoons red wine vinegar

3 cups water

1 bouquet garni (page 11), including a sprig of rosemary

½ head of garlic, halved widthwise

2 cloves

A pinch of crushed peppercorns

Makes 1½ quarts

(sufficient for a large piece of meat)

Preparation time: **about 10 minutes**

Cooking time: **about 25 minutes**

In a saucepan, melt the butter and sweat the vegetables for a few minutes. Add all the other ingredients and bring to a boil over high heat. Immediately lower the heat and cook gently for 20 minutes, skimming the surface whenever necessary. Unless you are going to serve the meat the same day, cool the marinade completely before using it.

Liaison techniques

Bread crumbs

Bread crumbs are used as a thickening agent for rustic, flavorful sauces. In country cooking, they are used to thicken the broth from a *pot-au-feu* or the pan juices from a roast. These are my favorite sauces when I cook at my house in Gassin in Provence.

Fresh bread crumbs: Crumble them into the warm sauce and cook very gently for about 20 minutes, whisking from time to time. When the sauce reaches the desired consistency, serve it just as it is, or pass it through a fine conical strainer.

Toasted bread crumbs: Crumble them into a bowl, and drizzle in a little olive oil plus, if desired, a small quantity of ground almonds. Mix thoroughly with a fork. Add the mixture to your warm sauce and bring to a boil over low heat. Bubble gently for 5–10 minutes until the sauce has thickened.

Egg yolks

Sauces bound with egg yolks have a velvety texture and delicate color. They always remind me of the creamy *blanquette de veau* that my mother prepared at home when I was a child.

In a bowl, break up the egg yolks with a very little barely tepid liquid: use milk, wine, chicken stock, etc. depending on the sauce. Off the heat, pour the yolks into the almost boiling sauce, stirring with a wooden spoon. Over low heat, reheat the sauce, stirring constantly, until it lightly coats the back of the spoon. It is essential not to let the sauce boil, or it will separate. As soon as it has thickened, pass it through a fine conical strainer into a clean saucepan and keep warm.

Cornstarch, rice flour, and arrowroot

These vegetable thickeners are quick and easy to use, need no special skill, and are ideal when you need a sauce in a hurry.

In a bowl, dissolve the thickening agent in a little cold liquid—water, milk, or wine—and pour into the boiling sauce. Simmer for about 10 minutes; the sauce will thicken almost instantaneously.

Heavy cream

Cream-thickened sauces are often used for fish, poultry, *veloutés* and certain soups. They add a velvet-smooth quality, which I love.

Always use heavy cream. You will need about 10–20% cream in proportion to the quantity of sauce. Boil the cream for a few minutes, then stir it into the boiling sauce.

The consistency, taste, and properties of heavy cream vary from country to country. For example, in the U.S., it is soft and delicate and can be stirred directly into the sauce and boiled without separating. In France *crème fraîche* is slightly acidulated and cannot easily be added uncooked to a sauce, or it will split.

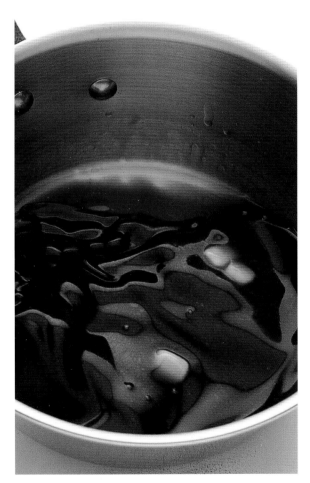

Lightening and thickening with butter

Incorporating butter into a sauce improves it in five important ways, making it lighter, smoother, glossier, thicker, and mellower. Once ready, these delicate sauces must not be allowed to boil and should be served as soon as possible.

The butter should be well-chilled, almost frozen. Take the boiling sauce off the heat and incorporate small pieces of butter (about 1 teaspoon), one at a time. Either use a balloon whisk or hold the pan handle firmly and swirl or shake the pan from side to side, until all the butter is incorporated.

Blood

Blood is mainly used as a thickener for sauces for game, such as venison and wild boar, or in the sauce for *canard au sang*. I use a touch in the red wine sauce that I often serve with duck at The Waterside Inn, and also in *civet* of hare, which is a favorite dish of mine.

Blood used for cooking almost always comes from pork, rabbit, or poultry (usually chicken). It is important that it does not coagulate; a few drops of vinegar added as soon as you obtain the blood will prevent this. Allow about ⅔ cup blood for 1 quart of sauce, or a little more if you want a thicker sauce.

Take the almost boiling sauce off the heat and add the blood, stirring continuously with a wooden spatula. Replace the pan over medium heat and cook the sauce until it thickens, stirring all the time. As soon as the surface begins to tremble, stop the cooking and immediately pass the sauce through a fine conical strainer into another pan. Keep it warm and serve it as soon as possible.

Swirl the butter into a sauce, a little at a time, to lighten and thicken it

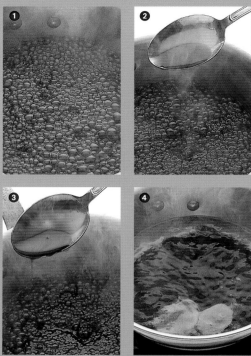

Reduction

You should be able to judge by eye when a sauce has reached the desired consistency by reduction, but it is helpful to use the back of a spoon to gauge the precise thickness. Let the sauce cool slightly before running your finger down the spoon.

Reduce the sauce over high heat to obtain the required consistency—a light juice (1), slightly syrupy (2), syrupy (3), or the very thick, rich *demi-glace* (5). As the sauce reduces, impurities rise to the surface (4); skim off as necessary. Never season a reduction sauce before it reaches the desired consistency.

Clarified butter

Clarified butter is used to cook meat over a high heat because it does not burn and blacken as unclarified butter would. It is also used for emulsified sauces like hollandaise and its derivatives and for making brown roux. During the clarifying process, the butter loses about 20% of its original weight. To make about ½ cup clarified butter, start with 10 tablespoons unsalted butter. Melt this over a very gentle heat and bring slowly to a boil. Skim off the froth from the surface. Carefully pour the liquid butter into a bowl, taking care not to include any of the milky sediment from the bottom of the pan. The clarified butter should be the color of a light olive oil. Clarified butter will keep in the refrigerator for several weeks.

Beurre manié

Beurre manié, or kneaded butter, is used to thicken sauces rapidly. Use only a small quantity, or the sauce will become too heavy. It usually consists of equal parts softened butter and flour, mashed together (uncooked) with a fork. Using a small whisk, incorporate small quantities of *beurre manié* into the sauce over high heat. The sauce will thicken immediately; let it bubble a few times, then as soon as it reaches the desired consistency, pass it through a wire-mesh conical strainer.

White Roux

This roux is classically used as a thickener in all white sauces.

Ingredients: *Makes just over ½ cup*

6 tablespoons butter   *Preparation time: 3 minutes*

½ cup flour   *Cooking time: 4 minutes*

Melt the butter in a heavy-based saucepan (1). Off the heat, add the flour (2) and stir in with a small whisk or a wooden spoon (3), then cook over medium heat for 3 minutes, stirring continuously (4). Transfer to a bowl, cover with plastic wrap, and keep at room temperature, or store in the refrigerator for several days.

Blond Roux

This pale roux is used to thicken veloutés *and sauces where a neutral color is required, particularly those for lamb, veal, and all poultry.*

Ingredients: *Makes just over ½ cup*

6 tablespoons butter   *Preparation time: 3 minutes*

½ cup flour   *Cooking time: 6 minutes*

Melt the butter in a heavy-based saucepan (1). Take the pan off the heat, add the flour (2), and stir in with a small whisk or a wooden spoon (3), then cook over medium heat for 5 minutes, stirring continuously (4), until it becomes a pale hazelnut-brown (5). Transfer to a bowl, cover with plastic wrap and keep at room temperature, or store in the refrigerator for several days.

Brown Roux

This roux is used to thicken many brown sauces. The clarified butter gives the sauce a deep color without adding any of the bitterness or unpleasant flavor of burnt butter.

Makes just over ½ cup
Preparation time: 3 minutes
Cooking time: 9 minutes

Ingredients:

6 tablespoons clarified butter (page 21)
½ cup flour

Heat the clarified butter in a heavy-based saucepan. Take the pan off the heat and stir in the flour using a small whisk or a wooden spoon. Cook the roux over medium heat for 8 minutes, stirring continuously, until it becomes chestnut-brown (left). Transfer to a bowl, cover with plastic wrap and keep at room temperature. The roux can be stored in the refrigerator for several days.

Recipes

- All meats are improved and enhanced by the addition of a sauce. Some, like game, pork, and rich terrines, pies and pâtés benefit from a refreshing, fruity sauce or chutney, which help to develop the flavor of the meat.
- Among my favorite sauces is that all-time great, poivrade sauce, whose satisfying flavor marries well with almost all red meat and game. I also adore Cumberland sauce, which adds a new dimension to a store-bought pork pie.
- White sauces are the perfect complement to poached or boiled poultry, white meats, and variety meat. Their ivory paleness or creamy whiteness make them appealing and easy on the eye. I particularly enjoy them in winter.
- Hot emulsion sauces like hollandaise are delicate and ethereal. Some, like béarnaise sauce are delicious enough to be eaten on their own. But remember that these sauces cannot be kept waiting, so prepare them just before serving.
- It is worth mentioning liaisons that require no recipe, such as a few caramelized onions, roasted carrots, or potatoes crushed into a sauce. Garlic or shallots baked in their skins on a bed of coarse salt make a lovely thickener for lamb gravy or the sauce from a pot-roasted chicken.

Roast turkey with Buccaneer's
sauce (page 35)

Béchamel Sauce

This is the ideal sauce for any number of dishes using white meats, poultry, and ham—even a genuine croque monsieur. The sauce will keep in an airtight container in the refrigerator for a maximum of four daiys.

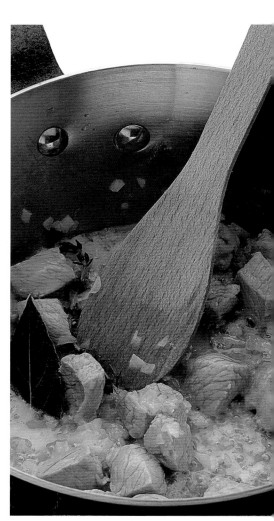

Serves 4
Preparation time: 5 minutes
Cooking time: about 25 minutes

Ingredients:

¼ cup white roux (page 22), cooled
2½ cups milk
Freshly grated nutmeg (optional)
Salt and freshly ground white pepper

Put the cold roux into a small, thick-bottomed saucepan. Bring the milk to a boil and pour it onto the roux, mixing and stirring with a whisk or wooden spatula. Set the pan over low heat and bring the mixture to a boil, still stirring continuously. As soon as it reaches boiling point, reduce the heat and cook at a very gentle simmer for about 20 minutes, stirring the sauce continuously and making sure that the whisk scrapes across all the surfaces of the pan.

Season the sauce with salt, white pepper, and a very little nutmeg if you wish, then pass it through a conical strainer. You can serve it immediately or keep it warm in a *bain-marie*, in which case dot a few flakes of butter over the surface to prevent a skin from forming.

Classic rich béchamel: The old classic rich béchamel was made with the addition of veal. To make this, sweat ½ cup diced veal and ¼ cup chopped onion, a sprig of thyme, and a bay leaf in 2 tablespoons butter. In another pan make a basic béchamel and when it reaches boiling point, add the veal and onions and continue with the recipe as above.

Aurora Sauce

Hard-boiled eggs sliced into disks, coated with Aurora sauce, and browned under the broiler are delicious. The sauce is also very good with poached eggs, pasta, cauliflower, or broiled turkey scallops. You can substitute a chicken velouté *(page 14) for the béchamel if you prefer the flavor. The taste of tomato coulis will vary according to the season; if it is highly scented and colored, use a little less. If it is pallid and lacking in intensity, use more.*

Ingredients:

1¼ cups béchamel sauce (opposite)
½ cup heavy cream
½ cup cooked tomato coulis
1½ tablespoons butter, chilled and diced
Salt and freshly ground pepper or nutmeg

Serves 6

Preparation time: **5 minutes**

Cooking time: **about 15 minutes**

Combine the béchamel and cream in a saucepan and bring to a boil over low heat, stirring continuously with a whisk. Bubble the sauce for 5 minutes, then add the tomato coulis. Bring the sauce back to a boil and cook for 5 minutes longer, whisking continuously. Remove from the heat and whisk in the butter, a little at a time. Season the sauce with salt and pepper or nutmeg, according to taste, pass it through a wire-mesh conical sieve, and serve immediately.

Bread Sauce

The perfect sauce to accompany roast chicken or turkey. It is also ideal with roast pheasant or grouse.

Ingredients:

1½ tablespoons butter
⅓ cup chopped onions
1¾ cups milk
1 small onion studded with 2 cloves
3 cups white bread, crusts removed, cut in cubes
¼ cup heavy cream
Salt and freshly ground white pepper

Serves 4

Preparation time: **5 minutes**

Cooking time: **about 1 hour**

Melt the butter in a small saucepan, add the chopped onions, and sweat them gently for 1 minute. Pour in the milk, add the clove-studded onion, and simmer at about 195°F for 20 minutes. Stir in the bread and bring to a boil. Lower the heat and cook the sauce gently for 30 minutes, stirring occasionally with a wooden spoon. Remove the studded onion, add the cream, and bubble the sauce gently for 5 minutes, whisking gently. Season with salt and white pepper and serve hot.

Parsley Sauce

This sauce is simplicity itself and most delicious, especially when it is prepared with the cooking liquid from a boiled ham and served with the ham. It also tastes good with plain boiled Brussels sprouts, carrots, or potatoes. You can enrich the sauce with cream or butter, but I prefer it without. Because it is not rich, it can be eaten with a spoon; this is why I suggest that the recipe serves four people rather than six, as you might expect.

Serves 4
Preparation time: 5 minutes
Cooking time: about 20 minutes

Ingredients:

1½ cups cooking liquid from a boiled ham,
   or chicken stock (page 14)
⅔ cup milk
3 tablespoons white roux, cooled (page 22)
2 tablespoons chopped parsley
A pinch of freshly grated nutmeg
Salt and freshly ground white pepper

Bring the cooking liquid or stock and the milk to a boil. Put the cold roux in a saucepan and pour on the hot liquid, whisking as you go. Bring to a boil over low heat, stirring continuously with the whisk as the sauce begins to bubble. Add the parsley and simmer the sauce for 15 minutes, skimming the surface with a spoon if necessary. Season with the nutmeg and salt and pepper to taste, and serve piping hot.

Supreme Sauce with Sherry

A classic supreme sauce is made without sherry, but I think it adds theatricality, which I like. Serve with poached poultry, sweetbreads, braised lettuce, or thin pan-fried veal cutlets. It is essential to use the best-quality butter to finish this sauce.

Ingredients:

1 cup boiling chicken velouté (page 14)
⅔ cup thinly sliced button mushrooms
¼ cup heavy cream
2 tablespoons butter, chilled and diced
¼ cup dry sherry
Salt and freshly ground pepper

Serves 4

Preparation time: **5 minutes**

Cooking time: **about 10 minutes**

Pour the boiling chicken *velouté* into a saucepan and add the mushrooms and cream. Simmer over low heat for 10 minutes, stirring occasionally with a wooden spoon. Pass the sauce through a wire-mesh conical sieve into a clean saucepan, turn the heat to low, and whisk in the butter, a little at a time. Remove from the heat, stir in the sherry, season the sauce with salt and pepper, and serve immediately.

Soubise Sauce

Perfect for winter, this sauce goes particularly well with roast rack or loin of veal and with roast chicken or guinea fowl. It can be prepared in advance and reheated in a bain-marie.

Ingredients:

3 tablespoons butter
1½ cups thinly sliced onions
1 quantity béchamel sauce (page 26)
⅔ cup heavy cream
Freshly grated nutmeg
Salt and freshly ground pepper

Serves 4

Preparation time: **5 minutes**

Cooking time: **25 minutes**

In a saucepan, melt the butter over low heat, add the onions, and sweat for 5 minutes without coloring, stirring gently with a wooden spoon. Add the béchamel, bring to a boil over low heat and bubble gently for 10 minutes, still stirring delicately with the wooden spoon. Pass the sauce through a wire-mesh sieve into a clean saucepan, pressing the onions through with a wooden pounder or the back of a small ladle. Add the cream and cook gently for 6–8 minutes, stirring continuously, until the sauce thickens to the consistency of oatmeal. Season to taste with nutmeg, salt, and pepper, and serve piping hot.

Sauce Albert

Sauce Albert, which we serve with our pot-au-feu, and cuts like veal shanks and beef flank, is one of the legendary Roux brothers' sauces, which our faithful regulars always enjoy. It is also excellent with roast rabbit.

Ingredients:

1¼ cups chicken stock (page 14), or broth from a pot-au-feu

⅔ cup freshly grated horseradish, or 1 cup drained bottle horseradish

1¼ cups heavy cream

1⅔ cups fresh white bread, crusts removed, cut in small cubes

1 egg yolk

1 teaspoon English mustard powder, dissolved in 1 tablespoon cold water

Salt and freshly ground white pepper

Serves 4
Preparation time: 15 minutes
Cooking time: about 50 minutes

Combine the chicken stock or broth and the horseradish in a small saucepan, set over medium heat, and boil for 15 minutes. Add the cream and bubble gently for 20 minutes longer. Transfer the sauce to a blender and whizz for 1 minute (you may have to do this in two batches), then pass the sauce through a wire-mesh conical sieve into a clean saucepan.

Add the cubes of bread and cook the sauce over low heat for 10 minutes, whisking continuously. Remove from the heat, add the egg yolk and mustard, and stir for a few moments before vigorously whisking the sauce to make it very smooth; it should have the consistency of oatmeal. Season to taste with salt and pepper, and serve at once. If you need to keep the sauce warm, do not let it boil.

Horseradish Butter

Finish a sauce Albert with this delicious butter, or use it to pep up a béchamel (page 26). It also goes well with any grilled white meat.

Ingredients:

¼ cup freshly grated horseradish

10 tablespoons butter, softened

Salt and freshly ground pepper

Makes just under 1 cup
Preparation time: 7 minutes

Pulverize the horseradish with a pestle in a mortar, adding the butter a little at a time. When it is all well mixed, use a plastic scraper to rub the seasoned butter through a drum sieve and season to taste with salt and pepper. Using plastic wrap, roll it into one or two sausage shapes, and refrigerate or freeze until needed.

Anchovy Butter

Use this delicious butter with any richly flavored game.

Ingredients:

2 ounces anchovy fillets in oil

10 tablespoons butter, softened

Salt and freshly ground pepper

Makes about ¾ cup

Preparation time: 7 minutes

Chop the anchovy fillets or pound them in a mortar. Using a wooden spoon, mix them into the butter and, using a plastic scraper, rub through a drum sieve or whizz in a food processor. Season, being circumspect with the salt because the anchovies already contain plenty. Use plastic wrap to roll the butter into one or two sausage shapes, and refrigerate or freeze until ready to use.

Caper Sauce with Anchovies

A lively, vigorous sauce that will cut the richness of variety meats such as brains, sweetbreads, tripe, or calf's head.

Ingredients:

2 cups chicken velouté (page 14)

1 bouquet garni (page 11), including

2 sprigs of savory

½ cup dry white wine

½ cup heavy cream

¼ cup anchovy butter (above)

2½ tablespoons small capers (chop them if they are large), well drained

2 anchovy fillets, finely diced

Salt and cayenne

Serves 8

Preparation time: 5 minutes

Cooking time: 15 minutes

In a saucepan, bring the *velouté* to a boil, add the bouquet garni and white wine, and cook gently for 10 minutes. Pour in the cream and continue to cook gently for 5 minutes longer. The sauce should lightly coat the back of a spoon; if it is not thick enough, increase the heat to as high as possible and reduce it for a few more minutes. Lower the heat to minimum and whisk in the anchovy butter, a little at a time. Pass the sauce through a wire-mesh conical sieve into a clean saucepan. Season with cayenne and a very little salt, stir in the capers and diced anchovies, and serve at once.

Champagne Sauce with Morels

This is the champagne sauce that I serve with poached capon. Try this unctuous sauce for a special occasion.

Ingredients:

3 ounces fresh morels, or 1 ounce
dried morels rehydrated in boiling
water for 1 hour
1¾ cups chicken velouté (page 14)
1 cup brut champagne
1 cup heavy cream
⅓ cup foie-gras butter (below)
Salt and freshly ground white pepper

Serves 8

Preparation time: **10 minutes**

Cooking time: **45 minutes**

First clean the fresh morels. Trim the very bottom of the stems, halve the mushrooms (or quarter them if they are very large), rinse in cold water to remove all traces of grit and delicately pat dry on a dish towel. If you are using dried morels, drain them from their soaking water and proceed as for fresh morels.

Combine the chicken *velouté* and three-quarters of the champagne in a saucepan and boil over medium heat for 20 minutes. Put the cream and prepared morels in another saucepan and bring to a boil over medium heat. Cook for 5 minutes, then tip the cream and morel mixture into the pan with the *velouté*. Cook at a bare simmer for 15 minutes, removing any skin from the surface with a spoon if necessary.

Add the remaining champagne, bubble the sauce for 2 minutes and remove from the heat. Add the foie-gras butter, a little at a time, mixing it into the sauce with a wooden spoon. Season with salt and white pepper, and serve immediately.

Foie-Gras Butter

This creamy, delicate, and tasty butter gives a superb velvety finish to many sauces, including allemande, Périgueux and port-wine.

Ingredients:

7 tablespoons butter, softened
3½ ounces terrine or ballotine of duck or
goose foie gras
2 tablespoons Armagnac or cognac
Salt and freshly ground pepper

Makes about 1 cup

Preparation time: **5 minutes**

Mix all the ingredients with a wooden spoon, seasoning to taste with salt and pepper. Using a plastic scraper, rub through a drum sieve or whizz in a blender. Using plastic wrap, roll the butter into one or two sausage shapes, and refrigerate or freeze until needed.

Sorrel Sauce

This sauce is one of my mother's favorites. Its hint of acidity and freshness makes it ideal for serving with pan-fried lamb chops or roast saddle of rabbit. A few shredded mint leaves added to the sauce just before serving intensify the taste of the sorrel and make the sauce more rounded.

Serves 6
Preparation time: 5 minutes
Cooking time: about 20 minutes

Ingredients:

2 ounces sorrel
2 tablespoons butter
⅓ cup minced shallot
½ cup white wine
1 cup vegetable stock
1 cup heavy cream
Salt and freshly ground pepper

Wash the sorrel and remove the stems. Pile up several leaves, roll them up like a cigar, and shred them finely, repeating until you have shredded all the sorrel. Melt the butter in a deep frying pan, add the shallot, and sweat it over low heat for 30 seconds, then put in the sorrel and sweat gently for 1 more minute. Pour in the wine and stock and reduce the liquid by two-thirds. Add the cream and bubble for 2 minutes. The sauce should be thick enough to coat the back of a spoon lightly. Season to taste, and serve immediately.

Rabbit with Sorrel sauce

Light Chicken Gravy with Thyme

This is the best possible light gravy to accompany roast poultry. It is also good with fresh pasta and leafy vegetables.

Ingredients:

3 tablespoons peanut oil

2¼ pounds chicken wings, coarsely chopped

`1 cup chopped carrots

⅔ cup chopped onions

1 cup dry white wine

1 quart cold water

5 juniper berries, crushed

1 garlic clove, crushed

A bunch of thyme, preferably fresh

Salt and freshly ground pepper

Serves 6

Preparation time: **15 minutes**

Cooking time: **45–60 minutes**

Heat the oil in a deep frying pan, put in the chicken wings, and fry over high heat until golden brown, stirring occasionally with a wooden spoon. Pour off the oil and the fat released by the chicken, then add the carrots and onions. Stir with a wooden spoon and sweat gently for 3 minutes. Pour in the white wine and reduce the liquid by half. Add all the other ingredients, being sparing with the salt and pepper, and bubble the sauce gently for 45 minutes, skimming as often as necessary. Pass it through a conical sieve; it is now ready to serve. For a more concentrated flavor, reduce the sauce over medium heat.

Zingara Sauce

Serve this fine, delicate sauce with pan-fried or broiled poultry or with veal cutlets, chops or scallopine.

Ingredients:

1¾ cups veal stock (page 12)

1 tablespoon cooked tomato coulis

2 tablespoons butter

¾ cup button mushrooms, cut in batons

¼ cup dry white wine

¼ cup lean ham, cut in batons

¼ cup cooked ox tongue, cut in batons

¼ cup fresh or preserved truffle, cut in batons

2 tablespoons best-quality Madeira

Salt and cayenne

Serves 6

Preparation time: **10 minutes**

Cooking time: **about 35 minutes**

Put the veal stock and tomato coulis in a pan and reduce by two-thirds over medium heat. Pass the liquid through a wire-mesh conical sieve into a bowl. Set aside. In another pan, melt the butter, add the mushrooms, and sweat them gently for 30 seconds. Pour in the white wine and reduce it almost completely. Add the ham, tongue, and truffle and mix delicately with a wooden spoon. Pour in the Madeira and cook at a bare simmer for 2 minutes. Add the reduced veal stock and simmer for 5 minutes longer. Season the sauce to taste with salt and cayenne, and serve at once.

Buccaneer's Sauce

I serve this sauce with veal chops at The Waterside Inn and garnish them slices of banana pan-fried in butter. You can serve poultry in the same way; the sauce and garnish go well with roast chicken (picture page 24) and turkey as well as with roast veal.

Ingredients:

7 tablespoons butter
½ cup minced shallots or onions
3 tablespoons minced fresh ginger
1 banana, peeled, and cut in rounds
6 tablespoons raspberry vinegar
1¾ cups veal stock (page 12)
Salt and freshly ground black pepper

Serves 8

Preparation time: **5 minutes**
Cooking time: **about 25 minutes**

Melt half the butter in a saucepan, add the minced shallots or onions, and sweat for 1 minute over medium heat. Add the ginger and cook until very lightly colored, stirring continuously. Still stirring, add the banana slices and cook over low heat for 2 minutes, until the banana softens and begins to disintegrate. Immediately add the raspberry vinegar and cook very gently for another 2 minutes, still stirring.

Add the veal stock and simmer the sauce gently for 20 minutes, then pass it through a conical strainer into another pan. Whisk in the remaining butter, a little at a time, until the sauce is smooth and glossy. Season to taste with salt and pepper.

Périgueux Sauce

This sauce is excellent served with little hot pies or pâtés en croûte, *with beef tournedos, or pan-fried saddle of lamb, and, of course, on pasta. For a richer sauce, substitute ¼ cup foie-gras butter (page 32) for the chilled butter.*

Serves 6
Preparation time: 5 minutes
Cooking time: about 30 minutes

Ingredients:

1¾ cups veal stock (page 12)
¼ cup bottled truffle juice, or (preferably)
the cooking juice from fresh truffles
2 tablespoons minced truffles
1½ tablespoons butter, chilled
and diced
Salt and freshly ground pepper

Use the juice from freshly cooked preserved truffles

Mince the truffles

In a small saucepan, reduce the veal stock over medium heat (1) until it forms a veil and lightly coats the back of a spoon (2). Add the truffle juice and cook for 5 minutes longer. Add the minced truffles and give the sauce a bubble. Take the pan off the heat and add the butter, one piece at a time, swirling and rotating the pan to incorporate it (3). Season the sauce with salt and pepper to taste, and serve immediately (4).

Périgourdine sauce: You can replace the chopped truffles with truffles sliced into disks or "turned" into olive shapes. The sauce is then known as *Périgourdine*.

Light Lamb Gravy Scented with Lavender Honey

This is a lovely sauce to serve with grilled lamb chops or a roast leg of lamb. Or do as we did as children—make a well in the middle of a pile of mashed potatoes and pour in a few spoonfuls of gravy.

Ingredients:

¼ cup peanut oil

2¼ pounds neck of lamb on the bone, coarsely chopped

2 heaped tablespoons honey, preferably lavender

1 cup coarsely chopped carrots

⅔ cup coarsely chopped onions

1 cup red wine

5 cups water

1 bouquet garni (page 11)

6 peppercorns, crushed

1 ripe tomato, peeled, seeded, and chopped

1 garlic clove, crushed

Salt and freshly ground pepper

Serves 8

Preparation time: **15 minutes**

Cooking time: **1 hour 15 minutes**

Heat the oil in a deep frying pan, put in the lamb, and fry briskly until browned all over. Pour off the oil and the fat released by the lamb. Using a metal spatula, spread the honey over the pieces of lamb, then add the carrot and onion to the pan. Stir with a wooden spoon and sweat gently for 3 minutes. Deglaze with the red wine and cook over medium heat for 5 minutes. Add the rest of the ingredients, being sparing with the salt and pepper, and bubble the sauce gently for 1 hour, skimming the surface whenever necessary. Pass it through a conical sieve; it is now ready to serve, but for a more concentrated aroma, reduce the sauce for a little longer.

The sauce will keep in an airtight container in the refrigerator for a few days, or for several weeks in the freezer.

Orange Sauce

I love this sauce served with slices of pan-fried calf's liver or sliced broiled kidneys. For a classic sauce for duck à l'orange, *I add some duck wings (when I can get them), which I brown quickly before adding them to the sauce along with the veal stock at the beginning of cooking.*

Ingredients:

' ¼ cup sugar

3 tablespoons red wine vinegar

3 cups veal stock (page 12)

Juice of 3 orange

Juice of 1 lemon

¾ pound duck wings (optional)

Zest of 2 oranges, cut in fine julienne and blanched

Zest of 1 lemon, cut in fine julienne and blanched

Salt and freshly ground pepper

Serves 6

Preparation time: **10 minutes**

Cooking time: **about 50 minutes**

Put the sugar and vinegar in a deep frying pan and cook over a very low heat to make a deep golden caramel. Immediately pour in the veal stock and orange and lemon juices and bring to a boil. (Add the browned duck wings, if using.) Lower the heat and cook gently for 45 minutes, skimming the surface whenever necessary. The sauce should now be thick enough to coat the back of a spoon lightly. If it is not, cook for a little longer. Pass the sauce through a conical sieve, season to taste with salt and pepper, add the orange and lemon zests, and serve. If you are not serving the sauce immediately, keep it warm in a *bain-marie* without adding the zests and add them only at the last moment.

Five-Spice Sauce

This sauce is excellent with a chicken baked in a salt crust, or with pan-fried veal medallions served with pilaff rice.

Ingredients:

½ pound chicken wings, blanched, refreshed, and drained

2 tablespoons peanut oil

½ cup chopped carrots

½ cup chopped onions

¼ cup white wine vinegar

1¾ cups chicken stock (page 14)

½ cup chopped tomatoes, peeled and seeded

1 small bouquet garni (page 11), including a sprig of tarragon

½ cup heavy cream

1 teaspoon five-spice powder

Salt and freshly ground pepper

Serves 4

Preparation time: **20 minutes**

Cooking time: **about 30 minutes**

Put the chicken wings and oil in a deep frying pan and brown over high heat. Pour off the oil and fat from the chicken, then add the carrots and onions to the pan (1) and sweat them for 2 minutes. Off the heat, sprinkle on the vinegar (2) and leave for 1 minute. Add the chicken stock, tomatoes, and bouquet garni and bring to a boil, then cook over low heat, skimming the surface whenever necessary, until the sauce lightly coats the back of a spoon (3). Add the cream and five-spice powder (4) and bubble gently for 2 minutes. Pass the sauce through a wire-mesh conical sieve and season to taste. Keep it warm in a *bain-marie* or serve immediately.

Curry Sauce

Serve this creamy, slightly fruity sauce with simply broiled veal scallops or chicken, garnished with curried or pilaff rice.

Ingredients:

3 tablespoons butter

⅓ cup chopped onions

2 cups pineapple, cut in small pieces

1 medium banana, cut in rounds

1 apple, washed and cut in small pieces

⅓ cup curry powder

2 tablespoons grated fresh or dried coconut

1¼ cups veal stock (page 12)

1 cup coconut milk

Salt

Serves 8

Preparation time: **10 minutes**

Cooking time: **about 30 minutes**

Melt the butter in a saucepan, add the onions, and sweat them over low heat for 1 minute. Add the pineapple, banana, and apple and cook gently for 5 minutes, stirring with a wooden spoon. Add the curry and grated coconut, then pour in the veal stock and coconut milk. Bring to a boil and bubble the sauce gently for 20 minutes. Pass it through a wire-mesh conical sieve, season with salt to taste, and serve immediately. If you wish, you can keep the sauce warm in a *bain-marie*; dot the surface with a few flakes of butter to prevent a skin from forming.

Bordelaise Sauce

This wonderful sauce looks as good as it tastes. It is delectable with any cut of beef, such as entrecôte, ribs, or sirloin.

Ingredients:

⅓ cup minced shallots

8 white peppercorns, crushed

1 cup red Bordeaux wine

1¼ cups veal stock (page 12)

1 small bouquet garni (page 11)

½ pound beef marrow, soaked in ice water for 4 hours

2 tablespoons butter, chilled and diced

Salt and freshly ground pepper

Serves 4

Preparation time: **10 minutes**

Cooking time: **about 30 minutes**

Put the shallot, peppercorns, and wine in a saucepan over high heat, and reduce the wine by one-third. Add the veal stock and bouquet garni and bubble gently for 20 minutes, or until the sauce coats the back of a spoon. Pass it through a fine conical sieve into another pan. Drain the beef marrow and cut into small pieces. Place in a small saucepan, cover with a little cold water, and salt lightly. Set over medium heat and bring to a boil. Immediately remove from the heat, leave the marrow for 30 seconds, then drain it gently. Season to taste, whisk in the butter, add the beef marrow, and serve.

Eggplant Sauce with Tarragon

Serve this creamy, refreshing sauce with roast rabbit, veal, or pork chops, or a dish of wide noodles.

Ingredients:

2 cups eggplant

2 tablespoons olive oil

½ cup minced shallots

¼ cup red wine

1¼ cups veal stock (page 12)

2 tablespoons heavy cream

A large pinch of paprika

1 tablespoon wholegrain mustard

1 tablespoon snipped tarragon

Salt

Serves 4

Preparation time: 10 minutes

Cooking time: about 25 minutes

Cut the eggplant into cubes (do not peel it). Salt lightly, leave for 5 minutes to remove any bitterness, and pat dry. Heat the oil in a saucepan and put in the shallot and eggplant. Cook over medium heat, stirring with a wooden spoon, until the eggplant begins to soften. Add the wine and cook for 3 minutes. Pour in the veal stock and bubble gently for 15 minutes. Add the cream and a generous pinch of paprika, then transfer the sauce to a blender and whizz for 30 seconds. Pass the sauce through a wire-mesh conical sieve into another saucepan, add the mustard and tarragon, and bring back to a boil. Season to taste with salt, and serve at once.

Venison Sauce with Blackberries

This fragrant, satisfying, but not overly-rich sauce is ideal with a roast saddle or gigot of venison.

Ingredients:

1 cup blackberries

2½ tablespoons sugar

2 tablespoons red wine vinegar

2½ cups game stock (page 15)

Dried zest of ½ orange

½ cinnamon stick

¼ cup Banyuls wine

4 tablespoons butter, well chilled and diced

Salt and freshly ground pepper

Serves 6

Preparation time: 10 minutes

Cooking time: about 40 minutes

Put the blackberries and sugar in a saucepan and cook over low heat, stirring with a wooden spoon, until the blackberries have collapsed into a purée. Remove from the heat, add the vinegar and give a stir, then pour in the game stock. Add the dried orange zest and cinnamon, bring to a boil, and simmer gently for 25 minutes, skimming the surface whenever necessary. Add the wine and cook for 5 minutes longer, then pass the sauce through a wire-mesh conical sieve into another saucepan. Whisk in the butter, a little at a time, season the sauce with salt and pepper, and serve at once.

Charcutière Sauce

A childhood memory...This homey sauce accompanied the pork chops and mashed potatoes that our grandfather and father served at their charcuterie in Charolles. If there was any left over, they would serve it to us the next day with a dish of wide noodles. I prefer this rather piquant sauce to have a slightly thick consistency, which I think complements the texture of pork.

Serves 4
Preparation time: 5 minutes
Cooking time: about 20 minutes

Ingredients:

2 tablespoons butter
¼ cup minced onions
½ cup dry white wine
1¼ cups veal stock (page 12)
1 tablespoon strong Dijon mustard
3 tablespoons beurre manié (page 21)
2–3 cornichons, cut in long, thin strips
Salt and freshly ground pepper

In a small saucepan, melt the butter, add the onions, and sweat gently for 1 minute without coloring. Pour in the wine (1) and reduce by half over medium heat. Add the veal stock (2) and bubble the sauce gently until it is thick enough to coat the back of a spoon. Whisk in the mustard and the *beurre manié,* a little at a time (3), and cook for 2 minutes longer. Season to taste with salt and pepper. Pass the sauce through a conical sieve into a small saucepan containing the cornichons (4) and serve it immediately, or keep it warm for a few minutes in a *bain-marie* set over low heat.

Juniper Sauce

This sauce is simple but highly scented, with a hint of muskiness. It is perfect with grilled or pan-fried steaks or lightly cooked game, such as pan-fried fillets of rabbit or medallions of venison.

Ingredients:

⅓ cup chopped shallots

1 cup red wine, preferably Côtes du Rhône

1¼ cups veal stock (page 12)

14 juniper berries, crushed

2 tablespoons red-currant jelly

3 tablespoons butter, chilled and diced

Salt and freshly ground pepper

Serves 6

Preparation time: **5 minutes**

Cooking time: **about 25 minutes**

Put the shallot and wine in a saucepan, set over medium heat, and reduce the wine by one-third. Add the veal stock, then the juniper berries and bubble gently for 15 minutes. Stir in the red-currant jelly and, as soon as it has dissolved, pass the sauce through a wire-mesh conical sieve into a clean pan. Whisk in the butter, a little at a time, season to taste with salt and pepper, and serve immediately.

Morel Coulis

Truly one for mushroom lovers, this coulis is excellent served with pan-fried medallions of veal or fresh pasta. You can substitute button mushrooms for the morels, but of course the flavoor will not be as fine.

Ingredients:

3 tablespoons butter

⅓ cup chopped shallot

½ pound fresh morels, finely sliced, or 3 ounces dried morels, rehydrated in boiling water for 10 minutes, then finely sliced

1¼ cups chicken stock (page 14)

1½ cups heavy cream

2 ounces cooked or canned duck or goose foie gras

Salt and freshly ground pepper

Serves 8

Preparation time: **10 minutes**

Cooking time: **about 25 minutes**

Melt the butter in a thick-bottomed saucepan. Add the shallot, then the morels and sweat gently for 5 minutes. Add the chicken stock and cook over medium heat for 5 minutes. Next add the cream and, still over medium heat, reduce the coulis by one-third, stirring occasionally with a wooden spoon. Transfer to a blender and process for 5 minutes. Pass the coulis through a conical sieve back into the saucepan, set over low heat, and whisk in the foie gras, a small piece at a time. Season with salt and pepper and serve immediately or, if necessary, keep it warm on a very low heat for a few minutes.

Chasseur Sauce

This light savory sauce is quick to make. It goes very well with poultry and veal.

Ingredients:

3 cups button mushrooms

7 tablespoons butter

⅓ cup minced shallot

1¾ cups dry white wine

1¾ cups veal stock (page 12)

1 tablespoon snipped flat-leaf parsley

1 teaspoon snipped tarragon

Salt and freshly ground black pepper

Serves 8

Preparation time: **10 minutes**

Cooking time: **about 20 minutes**

Wipe the mushrooms clean, and slice them finely and evenly. Heat half the butter in a shallow pan, add the mushrooms, and cook over medium heat for 1 minute. Add the shallot and cook for 1 more minute, taking care not to let it color. Tip the mixture into a fine-mesh conical sieve to drain off the cooking butter. Put the mixture back into the shallow pan, add the wine, and reduce it by half over medium heat. Pour in the veal stock and cook gently for 10–15 minutes, until the sauce is thick enough to coat the back of a spoon. Take the pan off the heat and whisk in the remaining butter and the snipped herbs. Season to taste with salt and pepper.

Savory and Tapenade Sauce

This sauce is very fluid, almost like a jus, *and bursting with the Provençal flavors of savory and olives. I often serve it with pan-fried or roast shoulder or leg of lamb. If you happen to have some lamb stock, substitute it for the veal stock.*

Ingredients:

½ cup dry white wine

⅓ cup chopped shallot

⅓ cup savory

6 white peppercorns, crushed

1 cup veal stock (page 12)

¼ cup black or green tapenade (olive paste)

2 tablespoons butter, chilled and diced

Salt and freshly ground pepper

Serves 4

Preparation time: **5 minutes**

Cooking time: **about 25 minutes**

Combine the wine, shallot, savory, and crushed peppercorns in a small saucepan, set over medium heat, and reduce the wine by half. Pour in the veal stock, reduce the heat to very low, and simmer gently for 20 minutes. Whisk in the tapenade. Then, still over the lowest possible heat, whisk in the butter, a little at a time. Season the sauce with salt and pepper, pass it through a wire-mesh conical sieve, and serve at once.

Exotic Sauce

This fruity, refreshing sauce has a light spiciness. It is particularly good with sautéed chicken or rabbit.

Ingredients:

1 very ripe mango

2 passion fruit

2 tablespoons cognac or Armagnac

1 cup veal stock (page 12)

½ cup heavy cream

4 drops of hot-pepper sauce

Salt and freshly ground pepper

Serves 4

*Preparation time: **5 minutes***

*Cooking time: **about 15 minutes***

Using a small knife with a flexible blade, peel the mango and cut the flesh from the pit. Finely dice the flesh and place in a small saucepan. Halve the passion fruit, scoop the seeds into the saucepan (1), and add the alcohol. Cook over low heat for 5 minutes, then add the veal stock (2) and cook for another 5 minutes. Pour in the cream, add the hot-pepper sauce (3), and bubble the sauce for 5 minutes, then transfer to a blender and whizz for 1 minute. Pass the sauce through a wire-mesh conical sieve into a small saucepan (4), season to taste with salt and pepper, and serve immediately, or keep it warm for a few minutes in a *bain-marie*.

Vineyard Sauce with Spices

Serve this sauce with roast pheasant or partridge garnished with grapes. If you prefer, substitute veal stock for game stock.

Ingredients:

24 grapes, peeled and seeded

¼ cup sugar

¼ cup Armagnac or cognac

1¼ cups red wine, preferably Côtes du Rhône

2 cups game stock (page 15)

1 teaspoon five-spice powder

1 small bouquet garni,

including 2 sage leaves (page 11)

4 tablespoons butter, chilled and diced

Salt and freshly ground pepper

Serves 6

*Preparation time: **15 minutes***

*Cooking time: **about 45 minutes***

Put the grapes and sugar in a saucepan, set over medium heat, and cook, stirring every minute with a wooden spoon, until the grapes have disintegrated into a lightly caramelized compote. Add the alcohol and ignite it, then pour in the wine and reduce by one-third. Add all the other ingredients and simmer for 30 minutes, or until the sauce coats the back of a spoon, skimming the surface whenever necessary. Pass the sauce through a wire-mesh conical sieve, season with salt and pepper, and whisk in the chilled butter, a little at a time. Serve immediately.

Light Chicken Sauce with Curaçao

This sauce has a very light consistency, almost like a thin gravy. I like to serve it with roast or pan-fried poussin or squab.

Ingredients:

2 tablespoons peanut oil

½ pound chicken wings and necks, blanched, refreshed, and drained

½ cup diced shallots

¾ cup diced carrots

½ cup diced celery

4 star anise, coarsely chopped

2 tablespoons Curaçao

1 cup chicken stock (page 14)

1 cup veal stock (page 12)

2 tablespoons butter, chilled and diced

Salt and freshly ground pepper

Serves 4

Preparation time: 5 minutes

Cooking time: about 30 minutes

Heat the oil in a deep frying pan, put in the chicken wings and necks, and quickly brown them all over. Pour off the oil and fat rendered by the chicken, then add the diced vegetables to the chicken in the pan, together with the star anise, and sweat everything gently for 2 minutes.

Add the Curaçao, cook for 1 minute. Pour in the chicken stock, increase the heat to high, and reduce the stock by half. Add the veal stock and simmer the sauce gently for 20 minutes longer. Pass it through a wire-mesh conical sieve into a clean pan, whisk in the butter a little at a time, season to taste with salt and pepper, and serve immediately.

Devil Sauce

This robust, highly scented sauce goes very well with all grilled poultry, particularly spatchcocked poussin or chicken.

Ingredients:

2 tablespoons best-quality red wine vinegar

½ cup dry white wine

20 white peppercorns, crushed

⅓ cup chopped shallots

1 bouquet garni (page 11), including 2 sprigs of tarragon

1¾ cups veal stock (page 12)

3 tablespoons butter, chilled and diced

1 tablespoon snipped chervil or flat-leaf parsley

Serves 4

Preparation time: 5 minutes

Cooking time: about 45 minutes

Combine the vinegar, white wine, crushed white peppercorns, shallot, and bouquet garni in a saucepan. Set over medium heat and reduce the liquid by four-fifths. Pour in the veal stock and bubble gently for about 20 minutes, or until the sauce is thick enough to coat the back of a spoon. Pass it through a wire-mesh sieve into a clean saucepan and whisk in the butter, a little at a time. Season to taste with salt and pepper, and add the chervil or parsley just before serving.

Cherry Tomato Sauce

This sauce is delicious served not only with pasta, but also with many grilled white meats. I greedily sup it with a spoon. It can be reheated very successfully and will keep in an airtight container in the refrigerator for several days.

Ingredients:

2¼ pounds very ripe cherry tomatoes, stems removed

1 teaspoon sugar

1 tablespoon snipped basil leaves

2 tablespoons ruby port wine

3 tablespoons olive oil

⅓ cup chopped onions

⅔ cup chopped celery

6 thick slices of bacon (about ¼ pound), diced

6 drops of hot-pepper sauce

1 teaspoon Worcestershire sauce

Juice of ½ lemon

Salt and freshly ground pepper

Serves 8

Preparation time: **15 minutes**

Cooking time: **about 1 hour**

Preheat the oven to 320°F. Put the tomatoes into an earthenware or enamel casserole with a lid and add the sugar, basil, port wine, and a little salt. Cover and cook in the oven for about 45 minutes, until the tomatoes have collapsed into a purée.

Meanwhile, combine the olive oil, onion, celery, and bacon in a saucepan and set over medium heat. Cook for about 20 minutes, stirring frequently with a wooden spoon, until everything is pale golden and well softened. Spoon off the excess oil, then mix the contents of the saucepan with the tomatoes. Transfer to a blender and whizz for 1 minute. Pass the sauce through a wire-mesh conical sieve into another saucepan and add the hot-pepper sauce, Worcestershire sauce, lemon juice, and salt and pepper to taste. Simmer the sauce for 5 minutes longer, then serve immediately.

Béarnaise Sauce

This sauce is wonderful with grilled steak and beef fondue. I eat it just on its own, spread on a piece of bread.

Ingredients:

2 tablespoons white wine vinegar

3 tablespoons snipped tarragon

¼ cup minced shallot

10 peppercorns, crushed

4 egg yolks

3 tablespoons cold water

1 cup freshly clarified butter (page 21), cooled to tepid

2 tablespoons snipped chervil

Juice of ½ lemon

Salt and freshly ground pepper

Serves 6

Preparation time: 20 minutes

Cooking time: 12–15 minutes

Combine the vinegar, 2 tablespoons tarragon, the shallot, and peppercorns in a small, thick-bottomed saucepan, and reduce by half over low heat. Set aside in a cool place. When the vinegar reduction is cold, add the egg yolks and cold water. Set the pan over low heat and whisk continuously, making sure that the whisk reaches right down into the bottom of the pan. As you whisk, gently increase the heat; the sauce should emulsify slowly and gradually, becoming unctuous after 8–10 minutes. Do not let it become hotter than 150°F.

Remove from the heat and whisk the clarified butter into the sauce, a little at a time. Season with salt and pepper and pass the sauce through a wire-mesh conical sieve into another pan. Stir in the rest of the tarragon, the chervil, and lemon juice, and serve at once.

Paloise Sauce

This is basically a béarnaise sauce flavored with mint instead of tarragon. It is excellent with roast or grilled lamb, and often appears on the menu at The Waterside Inn.

Ingredients:

1 quantity béarnaise sauce (above), made without tarragon

1 tablespoon snipped mint leaves

Grilled lamb chops with Paloise sauce

Serves 6

Preparation time: 20 minutes

Cooking time: 12–15 minutes

Follow the recipe for béarnaise sauce, substituting two-thirds of the mint for the tarragon. Pass the sauce through a wire-mesh conical sieve, then add the lemon juice, chervil, and the remaining mint. Serve immediately.

Parsley Coulis

*This coulis is delicious served with a grilled veal chop or chicken breast.
I sometimes substitute a pinch of curry powder for the pepper.*

Serves 8

Preparation time: 10 minutes

Cooking time: 8–10 minutes

Ingredients:

*9 cups curly or flat-leaf parsley,
stems removed*

1¼ cups heavy cream

⅓ cup thinly sliced shallots

½ cup milk, at boiling point

Salt and freshly ground pepper

Wash the parsley in plenty of cold water. Bring a pan of lightly salted water to a boil and plunge in the parsley (1). Boil for 2 minutes, then refresh in ice water (2). Drain, put the parsley in a cloth (3), and squeeze the parsley to eliminate all the water (4).

In a saucepan, boil the cream with the shallot and reduce by one-third. Add the parsley (5) and bubble for 2 minutes, stirring continuously with a wooden spoon. Take the pan off the heat, add the boiling milk and stir. Purée in a blender for 2–3 minutes, until very smooth, then rub through a drum sieve (6), using a plastic scraper. Season with salt and pepper. Serve hot, but do not boil the coulis once it has been sieved.

Port-Wine Sauce

One of my favorite simple game dishes is pan-fried pheasant breasts served with this light sauce. It is also excellent with pan-fried venison chops and roast partridge. For preference, I would use black currants, but since their season is short, I also use cranberries. These give the sauce a very slightly bitter tinge that is refreshing and very digestible.

Ingredients:

4 tablespoons butter
½ cup very finely sliced shallots
1⅓ cups finely sliced button mushrooms
½ cup cranberries or black currants
1 cup red port wine, at least 10 years old
Dried zest of ¼ orange
1¼ cups veal stock (page 12) or game stock (page 15)
Salt and freshly ground pepper

Serves 4

Preparation time: **10 minutes**

Cooking time: **30 minutes**

Melt half the butter in a small saucepan. Add the shallots and sweat until soft, then add the mushrooms and cranberries or black currants and cook gently for 3–4 minutes. Pour in the port wine, add the orange zest, and reduce by one-third. Add the stock and simmer for 25 minutes, skimming the surface whenever necessary. Pass the sauce through a conical sieve, swirl in the rest of the butter, shaking and rotating the pan, and then season to taste with salt and pepper.

Apple Sauce

Apple sauce is delicious served with young wild boar, wild duck, roast partridge and pheasant, or roast pork.

Ingredients:

1 pound apples, preferably pippins
⅔ cup water
1½ tablespoons sugar
Juice of ½ lemon
½ cinnamon stick, or a pinch of ground cinnamon
2 tablespoons butter
A pinch of salt

Serves 6

Preparation time: **5 minutes**

Cooking time: **about 15 minutes**

Peel and core the apples and dice them finely. Place in a thick-bottomed saucepan together with all the other ingredients except the butter and salt. Set over medium heat, cover, and cook for about 15 minutes, until the apples are tender but not dried out. Take the pan off the heat and, with a small whisk, whisk in the butter and a pinch of salt to make a very smooth compote. The consistency of the sauce will vary according to how ripe or green the apples are. If it seems too thick, add a tablespoon of water. Remove the cinnamon stick before serving.

Rich Pomerol Sauce

This rich, intense, and complex sauce is perfect with a well-marinated roast gigot of young wild boar. The perfect accompaniments to such a regal game dish are spätzle noodles, chestnuts, and braised celeriac.

Ingredients:

1¼ cups top quality Pomerol wine

1 quantity poivrade sauce (page 56), without the added butter

¾ ounce unsweetened chocolate, melted

5 tablespoons foie-gras butter (page 32)

Salt and freshly ground pepper

Serves 6

Preparation time: **10 minutes**

Cooking time: **about 25 minutes**

Pour the wine into a saucepan and reduce it by one-third. Add the poivrade sauce and simmer gently for 15 minutes, then whisk in the melted chocolate. Bubble the sauce for 30 seconds, then remove from the heat and whisk in the foie-gras butter, a little at a time. Pass the sauce through a wire-mesh conical sieve, season with salt and pepper, and serve at once.

Arabica Fig Sauce

This sauce is excellent with roast wild duck or squab. Fresh figs poached in red wine make a wonderful garnish. Be careful not to boil the sauce after adding the coffee, or it will become slightly bitter.

Ingredients:

6 very ripe fresh figs, each cut in 6 pieces

½ cup ruby port wine

1¾ cups game stock (page 15)

6 black peppercorns, crushed

1 tablespoon instant coffee powder dissolved in 1 tablespoon water

3 tablespoons butter, chilled and diced

Salt and freshly ground pepper

Serves 8

Preparation time: **10 minutes**

Cooking time: **about 40 minutes**

Put the figs and port wine in a saucepan and simmer gently for 5 minutes. Pour in the game stock, add the crushed peppercorns, and bubble gently for 25 minutes, skimming the surface from time to time. Add the coffee, then immediately remove from the heat. Pour the sauce into a blender, whizz for 30 seconds, then pass it through a wire-mesh conical sieve. Whisk in the butter, one piece at a time. Season to taste with salt and pepper, and serve immediately.

Pumpkin Sauce with Sweet Spices

This fruity sauce with its delicate flavor of spices is perfect with fillets of wild rabbit, noisettes of young wild boar, or pan-fried breast of wild duck served with a light garlic-flavored potato purée and crisply cooked snow peas.

Ingredients:

3 tablespoons oil

1 pound game trimmings
or chopped game carcasses

½ cup minced shallots

2½ cups pumpkin flesh, cut in small cubes

¼ cup raspberry vinegar

⅞ cup sweet white wine
(Sauternes or Barsac)

2 cups vegetable stock

1 bouquet garni (page 11)

1 vanilla bean, split lengthwise

3 star anise

1½ tablespoons butter,
chilled and diced

Salt and freshly ground pepper

Serves 4

Preparation time: *20 minutes*

Cooking time: *about 1½ hours*

Heat the oil in a deep frying pan, add the game trimmings or carcasses, and briskly brown them all over. Pour off the oil and fat released by the game, then put in the shallots and pumpkin and sweat them gently over low heat for 3 minutes. Remove from the heat and add the raspberry vinegar. After 1 minute, deglaze with the white wine and simmer for 5 minutes. Add the vegetable stock, bouquet garni, vanilla, and star anise and cook very gently for 45 minutes, skimming the surface when necessary. Pass the sauce through a wire-mesh conical sieve into a clean pan and reduce until it coats the back of a spoon. Off the heat, whisk in the butter, a little at a time. Season to taste with salt and pepper, and serve the sauce at once.

Poivrade Sauce

This sauce should be made with the marinade you have used for the game the sauce is to accompany. Poivrade sauce is rich and powerful and perfect for a large piece of game, such as a leg of venison, saddle of young wild boar, or roast hare or rabbit. It can also be served with pan-fried noisettes of venison. As these are delicate, you should not overwhelm the flavor with a very full-bodied sauce, so use only half the given quantity of marinade and do not reduce the sauce too much.

Serves 6
Preparation time: 20 minutes
Cooking time: about 1 hour 15 minutes

Ingredients:

3 tablespoons oil
1 pound trimmings of furred game
(e.g. venison, wild boar), cut in pieces
1 cup chopped carrots
½ cup chopped onion
2 tablespoons red wine vinegar
⅞ cup cooked marinade (page 17)
2 cups veal stock (page 12)
or game stock (page 15)
1 bouquet garni (page 11)
6 peppercorns, crushed
3 tablespoons butter, chilled and diced
Salt and freshly ground pepper

Heat the oil in a deep frying pan, put in the game trimmings (1), and brown them over high heat (2). Strain off the oil and fat released by the cooking, add the chopped carrot and onion to the pan, and sweat over low heat for 3 minutes (3). Pour in the vinegar and marinade and cook over medium heat for 5 minutes. Add the stock and bouquet garni (4) and cook at a bare simmer for 45 minutes, then add the crushed peppercorns and cook for 10 minutes longer.

Strain the sauce through a conical sieve into a small saucepan. Off the heat, swirl in the butter, a little at a time, until the sauce is smooth and glossy. Season to taste and serve at once, or keep the sauce warm, taking care not to let it boil. If you are going to do this, add the butter only at the last moment.

Grand Veneur sauce: Add 2 teaspoons red-currant jelly and 2 tablespoons heavy cream to the poivrade sauce to make a Grand Veneur sauce (this means "Master of the King's Hunt").

Quick Sauce for Game Birds

This quickly prepared but serious sauce is not too robust, but since it absorbs the savor of the carcasses during its brief cooking, it retains the full flavor of the game birds.

Ingredients:

2 wild duck, or 2 snipe,
or 4 squab
¼ cup cognac or Armagnac
⅔ cup red wine
2 cups vegetable stock
5 juniper berries, crushed
1 sprig of thyme
½ bay leaf
¼ cup heavy cream
Salt and freshly ground pepper

Serves 4

Preparation time: **5 minutes**
Cooking time: **about 30 minutes**

Roast the game birds until they are cooked to your liking, then remove the thighs and breasts, wrap them in foil, and keep them warm until ready to eat.

Chop the carcasses, place in a saucepan, and heat them through, then add the Armagnac or cognac and ignite it. Pour in the red wine and reduce it by half over high heat, then add the vegetable stock, juniper berries, thyme, and bay leaf. Cook briskly to reduce the liquid by half. Add the cream and bubble for 3 minutes longer. Pass the sauce through a wire-mesh conical sieve, season with salt and pepper, and serve immediately with the reserved breast and thigh meat.

Cranberry and Bilberry Sauce

I serve this sauce with terrines of game or pâtés en croûte. *It is also good served just warm with wild roast goose. The berries, particularly bilberries, can sometimes be rather tart; if so, add about 2½ tablespoons sugar to the sauce halfway through cooking*

Ingredients:

1½ cups cranberries
1 cup cold water
6 tablespoons sugar
1 clove, crushed
1 cup fresh bilberries or blueberries
Juice of 1 lemon
Zest of 1 lemon, cut in julienne
and blanched

Serves 8

Preparation time: **5 minutes**
Cooking time: **about 30 minutes**

Put the cranberries in a saucepan, add ½ cup cold water, the sugar, and clove, and cook gently for 10 minutes. Add the bilberries, the remaining cold water, and the lemon juice and simmer for 20 minutes. Keep the sauce at room temperature; it should not be served too cold. If you prefer a very smooth sauce with no fruit skins, pass it through a strainer. Stir in the lemon zest just before serving.

Index

Index

This edition published in 2005 by
Quadrille Publishing Ltd
Alhambra House
27–31 Charing Cross Road
London WC2H 0LS

Based on material originally published
in *Sauces; sweet and savoury, classic
and new* by Michel Roux.

Text © 1996 & 2000 Michel Roux
Photography © 1996 Martin Brigdale
Design & layout © 2000
Quadrille Publishing Ltd

Publishing director: **Anne Furniss**
Art Director: **Mary Evans**
Art Editor: **Rachel Gibson**
Project editor & translator: **Kate Whiteman**
Styling: **Helen Trent**
Production: **Rachel Wells**

The right of Michel Roux to be identified as
the Author of this Work has been asserted by
him in accordance with the Copyright,
Designs and Patents Act 1988.

Cataloguing-in-Publication Date: a catalogue
record for this book is available from the
British Library.

ISBN 1 84400 189 X

Printed in China through World Print Ltd.